Teamwork Makes the Dream Work

Life Source Scholars

Grades 3-5

Teamwork Makes the Dream Work

Written by the scholars of Life Source International Charter school grades 3-5 May 2017.

Published by:
Affirmative Expression
PO Box 360856
Decatur, GA 30036

First edition copyright © 2017, Affirmative Expression

All rights reserved. No part of this book may be reproduced or transmitted in any form or by any means, electronic or mechanical, including photocopying, recording, or by any information storage or retrieval system, without written permission of the author.

Cover by Chelsey Thomas
chels.t14@gmail.com

Printed in the United States of America

ISBN: **978-0-9963605-4-8**

Letter from the Publisher

The Anthology Project is a program created to provide a platform for voices to be heard. Often times youth feel their voices are not valuable. Others may feel pressure from the concern of their work being good enough for a passing grade. But while participating in this collaborative project they are able to speak freely with no concern for whether they will pass or fail. Most importantly, through the support of readers like you, their voices, stories, and efforts are validated and for that I thank you.

Tierica Berry
CEO
A Woman's Standard

When I created the Anthology Project it was to shed light on the voice of today's youth as it relates to various topics. Over the past few months I have had the honor and pleasure of working with the scholars of Life Source International Charter School.

These scholars were asked different questions about what success is and how to achieve it. During dialogue about this topic they were able to come together and write this book:

The Source to Life

Enjoy.

♥

Tierica Berry

CONTENTS

Chapter 1 Ms. Holmes   Pg 3

Chapter 2 Ms. Hackett   Pg 13

Chapter 3 Ms. Stearman Pg 36

ACKNOWLEDGMENTS

Before we begin special thanks must be giving to the people that made this anthology project possible.

Dr. Culpepper for seeing the vision and bringing the Anthology Project to Life Source.

Mr. Mix because under his guidance the project has been steered in the right direction.

The front office staff **Ms. Powers, Ms. Padilla, and Ms. Lopez** for helping to manage some of the fine details of this project.

Mr. Howard for assistance in scheduling.

Mrs. Mix for planning the book signing.

Last but certainly not least special thanks to the classroom **teachers** that worked closely with the scholars to complete their writing submissions. Without you this book would not be possible.

On behalf of Affirmative Expression and the student authors,
Thank You!

CHAPTER 1

HOLMES

Teamwork is when a whole group comes together. If you need help, say "Yes, I do need help." Say please and thank you for the help. Decide on an answer. Teamwork is good but it is not done. We still need just a little bit of work with each other. And need a little bit of ideas. Don't be mean when you are in a group. You got to be nice or you can just not do anything. I can say, "Do you guys need help?" Stop fighting over the answer, just vote for the best answer.

Cordell
3rd Grade

Being helpful and building off each other's ideas are all teamwork. Telling a group to think harder about good ideas is a type of advice to give to a team or group that needs help. Being helpful, caring, honest, respectful, kind and sweet is why teamwork is successful and great to teams and groups that need help, and even people who are not in groups. People should be thankful that they got help from people that are full of kindness and teamwork and have power to help people. Teamwork is great because people get their help and the courage that they can do anything they want to do for other people.

Kaimebreyah
Female
3rd Grade

Teamwork Makes the Dream Work

Teamwork is when a team works together like a family trying to win a prize, like $1,000. Oh, let me tell you a story. One day Tola was invited to a water park because she invented and made a Dry Through where you go to get dry at the water park .So they went their. Their parents went to go relax and all the kids went on all of the rides. And the manager came and told them that they owed $8,000. They had to work as a family to go into the champ games and the other team had won five years in a row. They had a big competition. The dad from the other team cheated so they had to step up their game. And the next one that they were doing was tug-o-war, so they went to go dry up at the Dry Through because the key to having balance is to be dry. They won the competition. That's how you work as a team.

The advice I would give to a team that was having a difficult time working together is "I know we are having a difficult time working together so we need to build off each other's ideas, and stop arguing. We can do this and we don't have to argue because we are all friends. We need to work as a team so we can win this. "

The most important things that make teamwork successful are not to argue, build off each other's ideas and make it bigger and stronger than before. So just work together to make things happen and work as a team, helping each other and saying nice things to each other. Make sure you are having fun because it is all just one game.

Tola
3rd Grade

Teamwork

Teamwork? It is mindful listening.
Teamwork makes the dream work.
Help working together as a group.
Make friends.
Don't be fighting and practice the game of life.
Be a leader. Be relevant. Be nice.
Be a friend.
In small groups you could give it a go.
You are important.
Be successful.
Be good in sports.
Respect others and solve problems.

Dulce
3rd Grade

Teamwork is when you work in a group. It also means you can help others with work and problems. Any advice I would give any group or person is treat others the way you want to be treated. The most important thing is to work together and get everything done. Also never forget to respect others. A story that happend to me is when my group and I were working in our workbook and we were goofing off, we only got a little bit of work done. You always need to be respectful body and mind. Also remember to show respect to everyone. Spread this message around.

Mya
Female
3rd Grade

Teamwork Advice

The advice is work it out and if that does not work just walk away. Teamwork is when you and your friend work together and be nice. Teamwork is just like me and my friends. We got into a fight at my old school because Meme, my friend, wanted my hot chips and I said no. So Meme got mad and then she walked away. The advice is to say no because if you say yes they will want more and more and more. The most important thing is to work together. You might be in a group with people you do not like and they are bullying you and they say you are ugly, but you know you're not, so you tell the teacher. That is right thing to do.

Destini
Female
3rd Grade

Teamwork

Teamwork is working in groups and helping each other, giving them a hand and helping them .
It is also working together putting in your best effort., being a problem solver asking questions and having mindfulness. Listening in teamwork...
Teamwork is helping discuss questions in a group, putting in your best effort and being respectful to others, always working together.
Putting effort is an important thing of teamwork. It is getting along and helping them out if they
need help and discussing it together.
Teamwork is believing in yourself, working together,
being a role model, putting your best effort, being respectful to others , being a problem solver.

Jocelyn
Female
3rd Grade

Teamwork Makes The Dream Work

If I see a team not using teamwork, I would say "Stop hurting each other. You guys are a team. To be successful, do not to hurt each other. You guys were born to success. Your all a family. You guys shouldn't hurt each other. Do you all know why? Because you are important. you're all important. In fact, the whole world is important. So like I said STOP HURTING EACH OTHER!"
The things that make teamwork successful is when everybody participates, asks, answers, and uses their brain. Do all of that and you should especially use your voice. Why? Because teamwork gives you all of that. So put together a team, so that team and you can use teamwork. Now your whole team knows how to use teamwork. Just how you showed them and everything that I just told you. All of it makes successful teamwork. Teamwork is everywhere; in your heart, in your brain, but sometimes you just don't know where it is in there. So use your heart, use your brain so that you can find teamwork. And trust me, it's in there, you just have to find it. If you do, use it. It's very bad if you don't want to. So please believe me and use it because it's true. You use it every day and I'm counting on you to use teamwork.

Josue
Male
3rd Grade

TEAMWORK MAKES THE DREAMWORK

What is teamwork? Teamwork is people discussing their problems in groups like teams, family, classes, etc. You need to focus on the goal by working together to solve problems. If you want something, you work together. They say two heads are better than one. You need to double check your work if it is all correct. You need to be a role model by having good ideas. Treat others the way you want to be treated. Build off of people's ideas. Learn off of people's ideas. Learn from others. Be on your best behavior. Use mindful listening.

I would give advice to a team in the NBA. I would say when you disagree with something you should make suggestions on what you want to do for your next game or pass the ball when surrounded by players to make a shot. When you use teamwork you can reach your goal by working together in small groups. It means to never quit. If someone thinks you can't do it, believe in yourself that you can do it. Be confident and stay focused. To be the best, train so you become better and better.

The most important thing about teamwork is to work together on what you are doing so when you have a problem, you can be an example so you can reach for you goals. You can use teamwork to accomplish something.

Rhema
Female
3rd Grade

CHAPTER 2

HACKETT

"Teamwork"

    I could help my team by telling them to not talk when they are in class and if they are mean I will say that is not nice to do things like that. If I had a team I would tell them about the rules to be nice about kids like myself. I would tell them about being a winner or a champion at all times because in life you have to be a good sport and a good person at all times. Sometimes when kids have to work together they don't want to do it because they might not like anybody in the group. Sometimes you need to be nice.

    Sometimes families, sports teams, classes, businesses will not get along, but you can get along with other people even if you don't like them. That is just how life is, sometimes you're okay and sometimes you're not okay because someone did something to you. So be a friend when somebody needs it.

    If you don't work with your team, you can make somebody mad or make yourself mad or sad. Kids might feel bad when you are mean. So be a winner and a champion.

    The most important thing to remember is being a team takes a lot of work. Some kids will not like others because they might not get along together at home or at school. I would tell them don't be a bad sport, be a good sport.

Amari
Female
4th Grade

Teamwork

What I would do to help a team that is having a difficult time is help them with their work. I would help them with their cursive writing or anything that they are working on. I would help them control their team and control themselves so their team can work together and stay on track forever and ever. I could help them if they are frustrated because they are not working together. They can make a better effort and get better grades. They could make the world a better place by being nice, helpful, kind, grateful, and generous, too.

Petunia
Female
4th Grade

Teamwork

Team: "Hey Guys"

Lisa: Hey guys, you know what we could do?

Elle: What?

Ashley: Ooh, I know! We could practice basketball.

Joey: Oh yeah, Ashley needs real help.

Ashley: Hey!

Alex: Guys! Can you stop fighting? Come on, we could all help everyone. Remember teamwork.

Jenna: I call team captain!

Nick: Me too! Let get started.

Jenna: I want Alex.

Nick: Hey! I want him.

Jenna: Ok, fine. You can have him. Elle come on!

Elle: Yay, I get to be on Jenna's Team!

Nick: Umm… Joey and John.

Jenna: Ally and Taylor.

Nick: Allen and Ashton.

Jenna: Donna and Victoria.

Nick: Jack and Sarah.

Jenna: Umm… Ashley and Mary.

Nick: Ben and Susan.

Jenna: Lynn and Rosie.

Nick: Why do I have to have Lisa?

Jenna: Because she's the last person.

Lisa: I want to go on Nick's team and that's the end.

Coach: (Blows the whistle) Nick's team has one point. Oh! Jenna caught up! Wow it's a Tie. Game Over!

Team: That's not fair. We Won! We got 3 points not one.

Coach: Hey! Guess what, at least you guys got to play basketball. Right?

Everyone: Yeah!! We got to play basketball!

Beautiful Dreamer
Female
4th Grade

Teamwork

One day there was a basketball team having trouble figuring out a plan for the game, but since the game was just about to start they started to scramble. When they were playing they weren't doing so well. The only reason they were doing bad was because they always argue and hog the ball. When they hog the ball they aren't using teamwork. When they learn to use teamwork it will help them a lot, they will be better and less argumentative.

The advice I would give that basketball team would be to try to work as hard as you can to figure out a plan because if you don't have a plan it might be difficult for you to understand what you are going to do. Another advice they could use is don't hog the ball and try to work together. Here are some important things that make teamwork successful:

1. Teamwork helps you to get batter.
2. Teamwork solves a lot of issues.
3. Teamwork helps you work things out.

Anniyah
Female
4th Grade

"Teamwork"

Advice that could help a group get along:

- Ask them what's wrong.
- Help them.
- Ask they that they just flip a coin!

What are the most important things that make teamwork successful?

- Stop arguing.
- Tell them there's no reason for fighting.
- Listen to your friend's ideas, then next time you say something.
- If your group wants to help, let them because they or you might start problems

    Some teams don't act like teams, they always fight for the ball or somebody is ball hogging. They need to learn teamwork like my team, we pass the ball a lot. I'm going to give 3 ways to make teamwork. First, you have to pass the ball. Sometimes if you can shoot it, shoot it! Second, they need to not argue all of the time. I would say whoever is the leader decides. Third, stop making a big deal out of stuff. He or she just needs to let it go.

Angel
Male
4th Grade

Teamwork

If a team is having a difficult time working together they can talk about the problem and how to solve it. They can try to figure out their misunderstandings. The most important things that makes teamwork successful is working together and sharing your ideas and answers to see if they're correct.

Teamwork Story

One day there was a basketball game and it was Teamwork vs. Hardy's. At first the Hardy's were winning. Then Teamwork was in the lead! So the Hardy's got mad and started cheating. They fouled and pushed. But they reason the cheated was because they just wanted to win. So the Teamwork team talked to them and the Hardy's understood that what they did was wrong so they stopped cheating and still won. The Hardy's and Teamwork's celebrated together.

The Last Strike

Once there was a boy named Leo, He was a baseball player. He always wanted to play in the major leagues, but they never let him on a team. Every single year he tried and tried. One day Leo was at the park where he practiced. A coach saw him playing and offered him a spot on his team. He said to Leo "Get three strikes and you're out forever!" Leo thought to himself for a second, then said "Ok. Deal." The day of the game Leo was in hitting the ball, "STRIKE ONE" said the umpire. "STRKE TWO," he said again. Leo got so mad that he hit the ball so hard that it broke a window. Leo had scored the winning run. Everyone screamed and yelled, "Leo, Leo, Leo." The team seemed amazed, yet curious. Leo is now officially on the baseball team and they all go out for ice cream.

E.L.B
Female
4th Grade

Teamwork

The advice you could give a team having a hard time working together is to use the golden rule, "Treat others the way you want to be treated." To work together you have to be nice and friendly to each other. Work together as a team in order for teamwork to work. The most important things to make teamwork successful are:

- To try
- To do the work
- To be friendly
- Have friends to do it with
- To be a true friend
- Ask nicely

Jazmyne
Female
4th Grade

"Teamwork"

One day on the football field the football players were playing football when a player saw another player fall down. So he went to help him get up, so that he could keep playing.

James
Male
4th Grade

Teamwork

Teamwork is when 2 or more people work in groups together. They can take a break then when they are ready to apologize they can be friends again. You can make teamwork successful by talking and learning more about each other and what you both like. Try not to fight because you might get into arguments.

De'Anthony
Male
4th Grade

"Teamwork"

Teamwork is working together with a partner and helping them calm down and not have a difficult time. Then they are going to be happy, they are not going to be mad at all anymore and they won't have a difficult time.

When I had to work with someone that I had a difficult time working with. Everyone in the group got mad at me.

Everyone has a difficult working with someone else and they might get mad at first because they just do not understand how to work on a team. If they get advice can be part of a successful team.

If I saw a team having a hard time working together I would try to make them laugh. I would ask them what's wrong and help them communicate with each other.

Jhenni
Female
4th Grade

Teamwork

I can help giving advice to a team by:

1. Helping them work together.
2. Being their leader.
3. I can give them advice how to work together.

That is how to help a team that is having trouble. The most important thing to make teamwork successful is to work together and be nice to each other.

Moji
4th Grade

Teamwork

Teamwork is when a group works together. A team should be nice and fair to people. Be nice to others. Be kind to others. Be good to others. Be helpful to others

Michon
4th Grade

"Teamwork"

Teamwork is a partnership. There has to be more than one person on a team. There has to be two or more people to make teamwork. You should not argue because that not ok. The team won't get anything done.

London
4th Grade

Teamwork

Teamwork is where you're working together and you're always a team. The advice I can give to a team is work hard, always stay together, and always be a team. The most important thing that makes teamwork successful is working together, always accomplish, and never give up.

Leandriah
4th Grade

"Teamwork"

You can work with somebody if they need help with their math or if they are playing outside and they get hurt you can help them up and make them feel better. If they cry you can make them feel better and be their friend.

You can work together and be friends and you should get your friend a job and you should work with her on that job. Then you guys can go to your friend's house together.

Saniya
Female
4th Grade

"Teamwork Makes the Dream Work Passage"

1. What is teamwork?

    Teamwork is when a team works together to finish their accomplishment.

2. What advise could you give to a team that is having a difficult time working together?

    Try to make a compromise.

3. What are the most important things that make teamwork successful?

    To make sure that you work together or things won't turn out the right way.

"Teamwork"

    A team decided that they were going to build a house, but one person wanted to start in the back. Another person wanted to start in the front. One guy said if we start at the bottom we can do both sides at the same time.

TRC
Female
4th Grade

Teamwork

The advice you can give them is take one person at a time and talk to them. Tell them not to aim at your teammate, aim at your goal. Goals like winning the game, pass the ball, take turns shooting, drive in, get on that defense, keep your hands up, put him on clamps, block shots, don't reach in, and just put him on clamps.

Shondrá
Female
4th Grade

Teamwork Makes the Dream Work

Teamwork is when a group of people who try to work things out. The advice I would give to a team who is having a difficult time working together is don't fight! Try and talk it out and if that does not work spend some time away from your teammates. When you're done and you have your head straight come back and say sorry to your teammate or team. Then everything will be back to normal and everyone will be happy.

Once upon a time there was a group and that group wanted to go camping. Everything was fine until they wanted to find food, but there was one problem. They did not know where to go. Jen said, 'We should go south." Jack said, "We should ho north." Jill Said, "No, you're all wrong. We should go west." Then Jim said, "I brought a compass, it says we should go east." Finally they all went east and they found food.

Joshua
Male
4th Grade

The Antidote

The forward for the Raging Bull's soccer team passes the ball to his teammate, who was wide open. The Knight Hawk's defender who was supposed to be there was arguing about position with the other defender. The Raging Bull's score and win the championship game. The Knight Hawks begin to argue and are told to go inside and wait in the principal's office until after the celebration.

Just after the celebration for the Raging Bull's an airborne disease begins floating through the air. The alarm from the loud speaker dings just before the principal announces,

"Everyone inside!" Then something else echoes out through the crowd...*Braaaaains*

Students and teachers start to scream and run for the school. Meanwhile the Knight Hawks; Frank, Alex, Rock, Ashley, and Patricia sit in the principal's office stunned by the news. Alex asks, "What are we all going to do now?" Patricia speaks up and tells them all about a secret passageway out of the school that is underground. Frank, Alex, and Ashley all agree and follow Patricia. As they run they find all the members of the Raging Bulls running down the hallway.

"Hey, look! The antidote." Frank points out.

"How do you know?" Ashley asks

"It says it right there on the bottle!" Alex says and they laugh.

"Hurry we have to figure out a way to get that antidote and save the world!" The Knight Hawks then have to work together in order to defeat the Raging Bulls and get the antidote. The Raging Bulls were going to destroy it, but the Knight Hawks saved the day. They give the antidote to the Army and they shoot it into the air and cure all the zombies.

Diego
Male
4th Grade

CHAPTER 3

MS. STEARMAN

THE BIG TEAM

Once there was a nice little school called San Diego Hills High School. There were seven kids who knew each other well. They went on a field trip with other kids from the school to go to the San Diego Hills College where they could see the inside and the outside. Everything about it made them excited and they dreamed of the college ever since. They all wanted to get a scholarship to their dream college where they wanted to be at ever since they were little. If the students wanted to go to college they'd have to pass the big test.

There was a problem and his name was Tyler. He was doing well in the beginning of high school but as the year went by he decided it was his chance to act like an animal. Seven years ago he was the prankster and a troublemaker at San Diego Hills Elementary. He got expelled for getting into at least 34 fights and he would sneak into the office to talk on the loudspeaker. Tyler was senseless, mean, and he was the bully of the school. We knew if he ever got into our college there would be a lot of trouble. Every time he did something wrong in our High School, he acted like he was doing a good job when any teacher would walk by. But it wasn't the same he turned our High School into a walking nightmare.

Our big test was coming up and we had to study

hard. One day when one of the students named Katie was studying, another student named Jake came in and said, "Let's go! You need to take a break from studying." Katie replied "I need to pass my test." Jake said "You're right I need to study too." So they studied together. Then Tyler came in the room and ripped their papers in half. Tyler laughed and said" Now you are going to fail the big test!" Jake and Katie looked at each other and got an idea.

Later on that day they met up with their friends Chase, Emma, Eric, Jaden, and Mary, to study for the big test. Everything was going good until Tyler walked in. He walked over to Katie and tried to grab her paper but everyone shouted "STOP!" Tyler was about to leave but Jake yelled "Wait! Why don't you study with us?" Everyone agreed and said "Yes! Join us!" Tyler shouted "NO" and walked out.

Tyler was mad the next day and didn't pass the big test but Jake, Katie, and all of their friends passed the big test. After the test they went out to celebrate by getting a pizza and ice cream at a famous pizzeria called Fun Zone. The next year they all got in their dream college, the next day they took a tour around their new college.

A.C.
Male
5th Grade

Team Work Makes the Dream Work

My family and I went camping in the forest. We brought friends and family. We were already scared when we got there, because the forest was creepy. While we were going, we told each other we would stick together as a team. The forest was creepy because it has a lot of trees and loud noises. That was the first time I had ever gone to a forest. Our hearts raced to our knees. My sister got so scared that she wet her pants. We laughed a lot. Then we heard a noise and ran.

At night it was very spooky. My cousins, friends, and I decided to run outside and face the monster and fight together all at the same time. We heard a noise over and over. We thought it was Bigfoot! Then we heard an even louder noise. We ran over to where the noise was, but we did not see anything. After the noise stopped we ran like crazy out of the cabin.

Then my crew and I decided to go outside in the dark without our parents. It was then that we saw a scary creature. As we ran, we decided to stop and throw rocks at the thing. We realized that it was just a little rat. The rat squeaked loudly because it was hurt. We helped each other out as a team.

The next day we went outside and the rat was still there. We thought it was weird. Then my cousin remembered that the rat was hurt. We went to check on the rat. It looked at us and ran away. As it turns out, the rat was faking the whole time.

That night, about midnight we heard more noises. Just like before, we ran out of the cabin without our parents. This time it was no tiny rat it was Bigfoot! We were throwing sticks and rocks and then we ran. Then Bigfoot said, "Guys get back over here." It turns out Bigfoot was one of our parents in a big monster suit.

That was the last day that we had on our camping trip. We put our hands in a pile and counted to three and shouted "Team work makes the dream work!" We were very sad to leave but we loved calling ourselves "The team-working cabin group." We thought for a second and decided that we can still be a team-working group, just not in a cabin going camping. Then when we got in our cars and said again "Team work makes the dream work!"

The End

Angel
Female
5th Grade

Teamwork Makes the Dream Work

The teacher put all the students in the classroom in groups of eight. In the first group there was Nancy, Stacy, Victoria, Iyanna, Jacob, Steven, Cory, and Jack. The teacher wanted to see how they would work together. They were all friends, but when it was time to do work they talked and argued for about thirty minutes.

When the teacher saw that they were just playing around and didn't have any work completed she decided to watch them talk about ideas. When the teacher walked away they started to argue again. The boys wanted to write about the Clippers, and the girls wanted to write about Golden State. They couldn't come to an agreement. When it was time for everyone to present their project they had nothing to present.

Their teacher decided to give them an extra hour to work on the project. Nancy and the rest of the group had to hurry up because time was moving quickly. Now one boy and one girl wanted to write about Golden State. When they finally stopped arguing they had only thirty minutes left. Stacy said "let's just write about Golden State." Three boys said, "No, that's stupid!" Now they only had fifteen minutes left. Iyanna came up with the idea to write about Clippers vs. Golden State.

Finally it was time to present the project. There was no arguing. Everyone got along and worked together. When you work as a team you can accomplish many things.

T-together
E-everyone
A-achieves
M-more

Byronaye
Female
5th Grade

Teamwork Makes the Dream Work!!!

Once there were two horses, one named Sparkle and the other named Buttercup. They lived on a farm. Their owners were always treating them bad, yelling at them and beating them. So, one day they decided to escape.

They tried to gallop away every single day, but it never worked. They started blaming each other and didn't talk to each other, and it started problems. They gave up on themselves. Then their owners stopped feeding and giving them water.

A week later Buttercup knew this was enough, so she decided to escape.

However, Buttercup knew she would feel bad for Sparkle. So, Buttercup went to Sparkle's cabin and said, "I'm sorry for blaming you for being loud when we tried to escape. I was just mad."

"It's okay, I was yelling at you for no reason," Sparkle said.

"So are we friends again?" asked Buttercup.

Sparkle said "Yes."

So, that night they planned their escape!

They decided to act like they want to stay, and the next week they would run away to a better home at night. They both like this plan very much.

A week later, the time had come. It was midnight, and they weren't scared at all. They were ready. So, they both said "I'm so ready for this!!!"

They started as if it were a race, and they ran just in time before the owners woke up.

They ran and ran and ran until Sparkle and Buttercup saw a great big barn with other horses and other baby animals.

For the rest of the night they slept close to the barn.

The next morning they went to the barn and blended in with the other animals.

But just then a lady came out with water and food. Buttercup and Sparkle wanted some too, so they reached out for it. But the lady said "Hey where did y'all come from?"

Then she called out to her family and said "Have you seen these horses before?"

They all said "No" and went back into a house close to the barn.

The lady didn't know Buttercup and Sparkle, but she still gave them some food and water. Then she took them into the barn to wash them off.

"I think I'll keep y'all," she said.

She treated them very well.

Sparkle and Buttercup loved it there, and the lady loved them.

They were there for a few months, so she wanted to call them hers. She filled out a paper saying she will take care of them for as long as she can. They were happy about it and lived happily ever after.

The End

Bilgiss
Female
5th Grade

When I Learned That Teamwork Makes The Dream Work

When I learned that teamwork makes the dream work, I was in 4th grade. I did not know any better. We did a lot of activities in that class.

One day, we were doing a class word search, and my teacher was picking groups. I wanted to be in the group with all of my friends, but instead she put me in a group with different kids. I got upset and did not want to work with my teammates.

My teacher said, "Get over here now!"

I got out of my seat to go see what she wanted with a big grin on my face. She said, "Why are you not working with your group?"

I got so taken aback because I was not in the group that I wanted to be in. I did not want to work with them or look at the other teams.

"They're working perfectly fine," said Mrs. Russell, "If you make a deal with me that you will work with your team, I will give your Mom and Dad a good report."

I asked, "But what if my sister Jessica picks me up today?"

Mrs. Russell replied, "I will tell her, and I will have her tell your Mom and Dad when you two get home. Now, I want you to go over there and work with your teammates. Look at row six. They're almost done. They could win. But you and your team have a chance to win too."

So I went over to my team and said, "You know what? I should have never treated you boys and girls like that. I'm so sorry! Let's get to work!"

Sometime later, Mrs. Russell told us that we had ten more minutes to work. Malvin and Erica said, "There's no point of doing it because we only have ten more minutes. We're going to lose!"

"No, please don't quit on me now! Teamwork makes the dream work," said Jack, "We only need two more words!"

"Now we just needed one more word, and we could win! See, it's not that hard after all! Now, let's get to work!"

"Look, look!" said Erica, "I think that I found one!"

"Yes," said Jack, "you did find one!"

"Mrs. Russell, our team is done!"

"Let me come check it," she said.

She came and checked it and said, "We have a couple of winners!" Then she walked up to me and said, "I told you teamwork makes the dream work."

And she said, "Here comes the good report to your Mom, Dad, sister, and the class, so they will know not to pull the same trick that you just pulled on me. I knew that you were one of the brightest kids in my class."

Byron
Male
5th Grade

Helping With Teamwork

There was a woman and her name was Stephanie. She was lost in South Carolina. Stephanie asked a lady, "Do you know where the fashion show is at?"

The lady said, "Yes I do. It is far away."

Then Stephanie said "what is your name?"

"My name is Cindy," said the lady.

Cindy said, "We have to take a train to get there."

Stephanie said "Ok."

Stephanie and Cindy bought two tickets. They had to wait until it was ten o'clock at night in order to catch the next train that was going to the fashion show.

When it was fifteen minutes past ten o'clock, they were still waiting. So Stephanie asked the lady who works there, "When is the train going to come?"

The lady said, "I do not know." Then they waited some more.

Stephanie and Cindy fell asleep for a little bit but were quickly woken up by the sound of the train. So they gathered all their belongings and got on the train.

There were a lot of people on the train, so they had go to the back of the train.

Stephanie and Cindy sat together and ordered food. Then they started to talk to each other. Cindy said, "We have a lot in common." Stephanie and Cindy became friends.

They decided to go to the fashion show together, but there were only four days left until it.

Stephanie and Cindy went to stay in a hotel. The lady who worked there said they only had two rooms left for the night. Stephanie said, "Ok." They got their own room.

The next day, there were only three days until the fashion show.

The lady that worked at the hotel asked, "When are you going to check out of the room?"

Stephanie answered, "I will get my stuff together and check out now if I have to."

Stephanie went to Cindy's room and said, "Open the door please."
Cindy said, "Hold on."

Then she asked, "Why are you not in your room still?"

Stephanie said, "I had to check out of my room early

because my room was reserved for someone else for the rest of the week."

Stephanie was really upset and sad. If she did not have a hotel room to stay in, she would not be able to participate in the fashion show. She had been looking forward to it all year long.

Cindy told Stephanie, "Don't be sad or upset. You can just share my room with me, and we can go to the fashion show together."

Thanks to the girls coming together at the train station, they were able to overcome all the obstacles that were in the way, and were able to have an amazing time at the fashion show together as a team.

Cynthia
Female
5th Grade

Teamwork

In class we're doing the Life Source Creed challenge in verbatim. The only ones left are Chance, George, Michael, and Devin. There were three in block one. Then we started arguing loudly so the teacher yelled "Silence!" So we stopped arguing. Then we stared at her. She glared back.

When the teacher left it got worse. We were yelling and screaming then someone lost their voice. We gave George two weeks, but we could barely hear him. So we gave him two more weeks, then he got his voice back.

Then Devin got injured at his basketball game. He broke his nose. We gave him six weeks, but his nose was still hurting. Then we gave him two more weeks, and then he was fine, but he could barely smell. So we gave him one more. He was completely fine.

We thought about it. After everything that happened, we formed a team. It took five weeks for us to recognize the creed, but it was worth it. The teacher was happy that we came together as a team after the big argument. So, the teacher let us have the ice cream party together. But we had to wait until Friday. When it was Friday, we had the party at the end of the day and everyone was happy.

The End

Chance
Male
5th Grade

A Story About a Story

Sometimes school work can get hard (like this), and you might need more than 1 person to do it (like this). Despite there being a lot of paragraphs you will be thinking you don't need help (you're so wrong).

So, say you're making a book that you will publish (like this). Once you write, you will have to check for grammar, spelling, and punctuation. Say you forget to do one step or worse all of the steps. Your reader won't even be able to read your book, much less buy it.

Which is why you need help.
So if you think about it, you will figure out that help is not bad.
You should let others help you, so don't say "No."

Now we're making a book as a team, and friends who are willing to help. When we write, our friends are constantly correcting us. Grammar done, misspells done, punctuation done. By the end of the day, when we all look at our papers, we will say, "We did well."

C.P.
Male
5th Grade

Teamwork Makes the Dream Work

Once upon a time a little girl who was sad and lonely. The girl's name was Isabella. She had no friends. She was talked about and laughed at because of her clothes and voice. Her voice was high pitched like a dolphin, and she couldn't get nice clothes, because she was poor.

One day, three girls named Jazmine, Taylor, and Katlin, wanted to be her friend. When someone was talking about Isabella the girls stood up for her. Then one day the three girls were getting talked about, and Isabella stood up for them.

The girls started standing up for more people and they became a team. One day, the bully of the school started bullying the team. The team was standing up for each other and telling a teacher and telling the bully to stop. The teacher told the bully to stop and the bully stopped and became a part of the team. The school became a better place in the neighborhood because of teamwork.

The End

Cahmora
Female
5th Grade

Teamwork Can Make a Dream Work

Last year I joined a basketball team at the YMCA and we lost our first game. After our first loss, our coach Joan said, "You guys need to communicate better in order to win games." So, we practiced harder on our communication as a team. The next game we played we communicated better.

It was 10 -7, The Roadrunners were in the lead. My teammate Hunter had the ball and she passed it to me. I shot and made a three pointer. Now the game was tied! We took a timeout so we could come up with a perfect plan. I was going down the court dribbling the ball, then passed the ball to my teammate Jacob, who drove in the lane and made a layup. That put us up by two points. Our coach said, "Hustle! Get back on defense!"

We got the ball back again, with only ten seconds left on the clock. I hit a buzzer-beater three-pointer, and just like that we were up by five points! The game was over, we won! Coach Joan started crying, because we only needed one more game to make the championship, and because she was proud of how we came together as a team to accomplish that goal. We reached our goal because of teamwork.

Finally, it was the last game. It was difficult, because we were losing. We were losing because we stopped communicating with each other. So we developed a plan because our coach said, "You guys are not working as a team." We started to communicate again and we started working as a team. We started catching up to the other team, finally started to pull away with the lead. We won the championship game and everyone started shouting. The ending score was 20 to 16. We were proud of ourselves as a team because we all worked together and won the game thanks to teamwork.

THE END

Dajuan
Male
5th Grade

The Donkey, Pig and Horse

The donkey, pig and horse were at a farm one morning. They were happy and wanted to play and have fun all day long. But this one horse didn't like being there because he felt like he was in jail. He tried so hard to get out. He shoved it, he pushed it, and he even ran into it with his head. Then the farmer heard something and came out.

The farmer yelled, "What are u guys doing out here?" They didn't say anything. After he left the horse said "Can you guys help me get out of here?" They said "Yes, but are you leaving?" The horse said, "Yes". All the animals replied, "Then we're leaving too. We animals are a team, and need to stick together." They all left with the horse. The farmer came back outside. He was so mad because all of the animals were gone. The farmer began to cry. He mumbled, "Goodbye".

All of the animals ran and ran until they couldn't see the farm anymore. After that they were free. They ate all day until they couldn't eat anymore. They traveled into the city and behaved like humans beings. They were never separated. People even thought they were humans. I don't know how they did, but that's what they thought.

Since the animals thought they were humans they decided to rent a hotel. All of the animals shared a room. They and started to have wild parties. The parties were so loud that the animals started getting complaints from their neighbors. Soon they got kicked out of the hotel. Unfortunately, they spent all of their money on the hotel room. They had no place to go, so they had to live on the streets.

The farmer went out to look for the animals. What the animals didn't know was that the farmer had a tracking device on their collars so he could always find them. The animals continued to play, without a care in the world. Little did they know that the farmer was on his way.

    One day, the horse was digging through the trash when he smelled a familiar scent. He looked up and saw the farmer approaching. The horse ran off to find the other animals to warn them. The horse said, "Hey guys, the farmer is here". They all yelled at once "What!" The horse said "Quick, let's get out of here". They started to run. The Donkey asked, "How did he find us?" The horse replied, "I don't know". They looked back to ask pig something, but they noticed that the farmer had caught up with the pig. The donkey and the horse rushed back and attacked the farmer. They weren't going to let the farmer take their friend back to that old barnyard. They managed to get the pig away from the farmer. Then they ran as fast as they could. The farmer never caught up with them. They worked as a team to escape the farmer twice. Teamwork made the dream work.

The End.

IYANNA
FEMALE
5TH GRADE

Teamwork With Family

Once upon a time there was the Mack family and their Pitbull. They had a competition with some other families; they called it the family Olympics. Our family worked together as team. My dad passed me the football and I ran straight to Little Bob and broke his ankles. My mom and sister worked together to win the handstand race. They were going against the Williams family and their mixed collie dog. The dads, Eric and Bob, went first. When they got to the starting line they took off running my dad was ahead by a little bit and won the race. He touched my hand and I took off running as fast as I could. Little Bob was catching up to me, so I started to run even harder! Then the Williams family stopped using teamwork. The dogs had to race two times because the first race was a tie. On the second race the Pitbull Benzie won the race. The Collie, Tessey, was sad that she didn't win.

The Mack family got to move on in the competition. It was the Mack family vs the Dickerson family, but this time it was just the dogs and sons. I was far behind Mike. My dad said "If we want to win we have to use teamwork." I had catch up to Mike. We had to do 2 laps. Mike was too tired to run faster and ran out of breath. Mike stopped to breathe and I snuck past him. I was finally on my last lap. I got to our dog, Benzie, and pulled his tail to run. Mike was right there to pull Belly's tail. Belly took off running. Benzie woke up and start running. The crowd was happy. Then Benzie started catching up. He pulled ahead by a

head. At the finish line Benzie stuck his dried tongue out and won.
Belly and Benzie fell in love. Belly had puppies.
There was a conflict with the families about who was taking which puppies. The Mack's took Little Benzie, Baby Belly, Tyson, Kaydo and Missy. The Dickersons got Max, Tanc, King, Suzy and Tiny.
Belly had a surprise puppy when everybody was talking. All the parents turned their heads and saw a puppy coming out. They all fainted on the floor.
Belly had eleven puppies total. Benzie supported Belly every step of the way. He got warm towels for Belly and helped clean the puppies up. They worked together as a team to help the puppies.

Eric
Male
5th Grade

The Great Piggy Power

Once there were three little pigs. They never loved each other. All though they were siblings, they never loved living in the same house. In fact they always stayed in their rooms unless they were getting something to eat. They made sure to all eat at different times.

Every weekend they had a family meeting, which they hated. One piggy said, "That's it, if we want to get separate house's we are going to have to work for it." After that speech their lives changed forever.

They all tried to work at the same place. They got the job but it did not work at all. So, they tried different jobs. That worked and finally the moment they have all have been waiting for, jobs at McDonalds. They did not want to go to one job, but they only had one car. So one job it was.

The cooking piggy was making the fries, the grouchy piggy cleaned the toilets, and nicest piggy of all that had the best of the jobs. He got the job as a cashier and he loved it!

They didn't make much money. So, they worked as a team and saved their money together. When they had enough money for only one of them to get a home, they fought. They fought about the money every single day and at their job also. So they asked the manager and each got their own separate money. Then they had to demand the manager to pay them more money.

They got their own money and a couple of

extra dollars. They kept working for enough money to buy their own cars or trucks. One day they decided to look for other jobs, because McDonald's jobs are only OK.

When they had enough money they looked for jobs like working for celebrities, but you had to pay for that. That is why they saved up so they got good jobs and better lives. Now they have their own homes, cars, and jobs but they were all sad that all the three brothers did not see each other. So they decided to have a family meeting every day in their old home.

They loved it then. That's how they lived their lives and kept working to get their own cars. After that they helped each other move their furniture into their own homes and they always remembered that it was teamwork that got them what they wanted.

Emyliana
Female
5th Grade

Teamwork

Roy and his friends were at school one day and they had a science project to do on natural disasters. Roy, Terrance, and Blake were picked to be partners. When they got to Roy's house they tried to decide what to do it on. Roy suggested they do it on hurricanes, but Terrance and Blake did not agree. The boys started arguing about what to do their project on, before finally agreeing to do it on earthquakes.

The next day after school was over the group went to Roy's house to begin working on their project, but quickly realized that they did not have any supplies. They went to ask Roy's dad to take them to the store to buy the supplies they would need. They bought clay, glue, sticks, scissors, and construction paper and also had to print out facts about earthquakes. When they got back they got to work. Roy glued the facts, Terrance did the modeling, and Blake did the cutting. The boys did not complete their project but thankfully it was not due until Friday.

The next day there was no school so they all met up together to pick up where they left off and had all day to finish but, they started playing video games until one o'clock and forgot about their project. They got working to try to get it done but they went slow so they could try to edit it, But Blake keep playing the video game and lost the sticks. They were frustrated and blamed it on Blake because he was supposed to keep the sticks with him. They finally found the sticks the next day which was now Wednesday.

Roy, Terrance, and Blake were working hard on Thursday. They balanced the sticks and pushed them into the clay model. They worked on and on until Roy accidently tripped and fell down a couple stairs at his house while he was holding the clay model and it broke. Roy was hurt bad but Blake and Terrance were mad at Roy for breaking their project. When Roy fell he broke his foot so he could not get around as easy as before. The guys put their frustrations aside and met up with each other at Roy's house and fixed the project together in Roy's bedroom so that he did not have to move around that much with his broken foot. They worked long and hard but finally got it done.

Before they went home they checked the model for no broken pieces. The next day they turned it in. Later they were supposed to present their project but they got scared and ran to their seats. They presented it only to Mrs. Amerson. They got a B, they were happy with how well they did after finally coming together and completing the project as a team. That next weekend the group of boys met up again and ate pizza and they had happy day at Roy's house playing video games.

Diego B.
Male
5th Grade

The Dreamers

James, Jarod, and Chance had a group made to help others win. James is the captain of the group, because he is the one who brought it up. He hates seeing other scholars fail or being lonely.

So one day, he came up to Chance and Jarod and said, "Do you guys want to be a part of the group I made to help others win, like us?"

Chance said "Hmm."

Jarod said, in his mind, "Nope."

Then Chance said out loud, "Sure, why not!"

James was surprised that they said yes, even Jarod, as they put their hands in and all yelled "DREAMERS!"

They all went to pick up trash around the whole school.

James went to the dirtiest place he ever saw in his life, the bleachers. But Jarod and Chance went and looked for trash nearby.

The next day at school, they made posters that said "Teamwork is the key," and put them all over to make other scholars help out.

A couple of hours later, it was free-play, and James said, "Go help someone that is sitting somewhere being lonely."

Jarod replied, "Yes," as Chance and James ran off because Jarod loves helping lonely people more than James and Chance.

After free play was over they told how many people they played and became friends with.

Jarod got ten people, James got nine people, and Chance got eleven people!

After school was over the Dreamers saw a guy picking on another kid. They ran over there and told the guy, "Stop! Leave him alone!"

The guy replied, "Be quiet, or your next, Shorty!"

After that, they told a teacher.

The next day, after school started, a new team had been created to make some money at school called "scholar dollars". The Dreamers joined it and noticed that it was fake. It was actually a bullying group called "The Hammers". So, the Dreamers went back to business and left The Hammers.

At free-play, James said, "Turning in the bullies will be the last thing for us to do."

They put their hands in, and said "Dreamers." Then they split up.

There were only three bullies, and they turned them in one-by-one.

When they finished the last quest, they retired, making about five million scholar dollars from doing that.

James
Male
5th grade

"TEAMWORK MAKES THE DREAM WORK"

Teamwork Makes the Dream Work is helping others with work, and you will get a lot of a work done. You will be successful, and you will graduate from high school and other grades.

If you have teamwork, things will work out well, and that is what makes you dream to do anything you want in the future. You can buy phones and stuff like that.

In minecraft, my dad, Ziyah and I were all building together, and we got a lot of work done. I'm talking about work. It was eight times bigger than the clouds, and it was almost touching the moon!

On Battle Mini-games Minecraft, I had to help Ziyah and Jayla in the game, and we really won!

Teamwork is so awesome! It's like being an elite team!

It's like having someone giving too much credit for your home work! And it'll feel like you finished anything!

The Avengers work together to defeat any other enemy. In "Captain America: Civil War", they all broke up and made another team.

Captain America's team won, because they never gave up. He told them to keep on going, no matter what.

When you work together, you all might have different ideas. So you might argue, but sometimes you need to let it go for the good of the team.

Kahlil
Male
5th Grade

Teamwork

One day there was a teenage girl named Nevaeh Caldwell. She was new to Lancaster High School, and she was in the 10th grade.

On her second day, she was going to Wing Stop to get some wings. While she was going to her car, a group of girls, named Kennedy (the leader), Keshia (the guard dog) and Barbara (the bully), all walked up to Nevaeh and said, "Look at that dork, she looks like a loner." Then they all started laughing.

While the girls kept on talking about Nevaeh, a girl named Heavenly came over and said, "Hey, stop bothering her! She's just new."

Then the girls came over towards her and started pushing her. Then they dragged her by a locker, gave her a wedgie and laughed at her.

Nevaeh went to the locker, thanked her twenty thousand times, got her off the locker, and then took her to the office.

After they came back from the office, they started hanging out with each other every single day.

Then they started to get more friends to

overcome the bullies. Their whole group was able to beat them, and so they did. And after that the bullies never bullied them again.

The next day there were only two of the girls. Jasmine, Victoria and the other girls asked, "What happened to Janayah?"

"Well, we were on our way to Chipotle, and we were crossing the street. She told us there was a car coming, but Barbara and I were too busy talking to hear her. So Janayah jumped in front of us, and now she's in the hospital," said Kennedy.

Nevaeh said, "I feel sad for her and her family, but at least she's getting the help she needs."

After Janayah came back from the hospital, all the girls became best friends.

THE END

Jordyn
5th Grade

Team Work Angels

    This girl named Sandy was new at her school. Actually, it was her first day. A girl named Sam came along and said to Sandy, "Hi, do you want to be on the soccer team?" Sandy said, "Sure, why not?" Sam was excited. Sam said to Sandy, "Oh and there aren't any boys on the team, just girls." Sandy was really excited about joining the Angels. She was so good at the game that they made her the goalie.
    Sam told Sandy everything about the team. Sam also warned Sandy about their rival team, The Stealers. "That team's leader is a stealer", said Sam. "Watch out for Linda. She always steals the ball."
    Sandy and the Angels always played their best. However, they lost at times. After one particular loss, the team went into the locker room. Candy, the Angels team leader, said, "We can try harder next time. Remember teamwork." Then everybody started chanting "Teamwork, teamwork, teamwork." Coach Ronald came in and said, "We will practice very hard, and do better next game."
    The next day, Sandy woke up and put her soccer outfit on for practice. When she got there she didn't see Candy. When Sam came, she saw Sandy and went to her. She told her what happened to Candy. She said that Candy got sick and couldn't come to practice. Then the team got an idea to put Sandy in charge. Sandy was really

happy and said "Ok, I will do it."

They practiced really hard everyone messed up a little, but everybody still did well. With Sandy in charge, they practice so hard that everybody did well and they won the big game. They went against their enemy the Stealers. When they won the trophy they had a party at Sam's house everybody chanted, Sandy, Sandy, Sandy, Sandy. Sandy came to the front and said, "We wouldn't have won without teamwork. Teamwork had to be why we won, when we have a big game we will always have teamwork. Anywhere we go it will always be with us." When they have practice or a big game, they will always use teamwork in every game. Now they win every game and became the worldwide champions of the, women's soccer team.

The End

Jenna
Female
5th Grade

Teamwork Makes the Dream Work

One day, a group of boys were at a park. There were exactly ten people. They wanted to play a full-court basketball game. There were always two team captains that pick back and forth who they want on their team. Everybody wanted to be team captain. Then the oldest boy, John, said, "I'm team captain, because I am the oldest!" And everybody else started arguing over who should be team captain.

The youngest boy, Anthony, said, "Let's have a shooting contest, and whoever wins, they are team captain." Everybody agreed with it. First up were John and Byron. "Best out of ten shots wins," Anthony said. John won the first round and went against James. John won the second round and moved on.
He kept on winning until he got down to one more person. So that meant John and Anthony were both team captains. After they picked their teams, they went to both sides of the court. Then the two teams both gathered in a huddle. After they ended their planning, the two teams both put their hands on top of each other's.

Then, when they went to the court, Anthony remembered something. "Hey, who is going to jump for the basketball?" Then another commotion happened over who was going to jump. They were yelling loudly.
Then one of the stronger kids, Miles, said, "Let the team captains jump for the ball." Not everybody was happy about that.

Another kid, Amere, exclaimed, "Anthony is too little, and John will win the jump!"
John, a thoughtful kid said, "Let's just let Anthony's team start with the ball. I mean, we do have a good team, you know."
Everybody just went with it. So then they finally had their game, and there were no more arguments.

Jarod
Male
5th Grade

The General and His Army

Once there was a General that wanted to win wars, but his army would not work together. When someone was about to shoot, someone took the gun.
They would often fight each other. One day the General got tired of dealing with it, so he said, "Do you want to win wars or not!"
They lost more and more wars. Eventually though they started liking teamwork. Then the General came, and he was pleased in how they were working as a team. So, he bought them a pizza, and gave them time to talk to their families. Eventually everyone became Generals, and it was all because of teamwork.

Kavali
Male
5th Grade

Teamwork Makes the Dream Work

At my baseball game I had to get one more point or we wouldn't have won. My teammate at 3rd base ran and made the point. However, it did not count because he didn't touch the base. So, we had to get on the field. Bill wanted to be the first-baseman, but I was. We had about fifteen minutes to go and he got mad. He hit me, so the team came out to help and everyone said, "Stop!" Then coach said, "Stop and get in the game. Bill said, "I'm first base!" So I said, "Back off it's mine!" We didn't see that five people ran past us and won the game. So coach gave us an idea he said," Mekhi, first base is yours for today and Bill, you're first base the next day."

The next season coach put me on 3rd base and my friend on first. He was bad at his job, he couldn't catch the ball when they threw it to him. So my coach put him to right field. He had to catch the ball when it gets hit to the right field. It was our last game for the week and our best player Isaiah wasn't there, so I had to help my team win by leading them. We won and the score was sixteen to nineteen. We had a party at Vincent Pasta and Pizza.

We got back from the party and went home but a lot of coaches wanted to have a game with us. We grabbed our baseball clothes. We got to the field and it was a set up. My coach said, "All of the teams are going against another," and they said, "Choose your teammate." They ran to me and my friend Isaiah and said "Please can I be on your team?" I Said "No get lost!" I chose Isaiah and we won the game. Me and Isaiah said, "You guy are weak." Coach said, "Good job!" The other kid was on the floor saying "You guys are mean!" They called us names and our teammates who were at the snack bar ran to us and we solved the problem. We were off our game all week and we just needed to believe that we can win.

Me'khi
Male
5th Grade

The New Family House

One warm early morning, a day everyone wanted to play outside, the Hawes family decided to have a yard sale for the first time. They wanted to work together as a team to get money so the family can move into a house with an outdoor pool in the back yard. The mother started selling dresses and heels, the twins, Ally and Grace are going to sell the toys and small tables, and their Dad was selling dog beds.

If they sold all those things they will have about $3,000 dollars. The house they wanted was $5,000. They were trying their best to work together to get the house they wanted. Dad said, "It's getting late." So everybody started to clean up and went inside to take showers for the next day. There were only two bathrooms, one in the hallway and one in the parent's room. It would be hard for everyone to get a shower before bed time, but everyone worked together as a good team and they finished the showers just in time for bed.

Teamwork Makes the Dream Work

Like all good teams they quickly set up for the sale the next day. They just finished setting up when it started softly raining.

Mom wasn't going to give up, so she decided to have the sale in the garage.

They made $4997, and only needed three more dollars. Nobody else was coming because they didn't want to be in the rain.

They was about to quit when mom saw Howey, Grace's friend. They was very happy to see him, because he bought some heels.

Mom ask him why he bought heels. He said, "They're for my mom." She said, "OK, that's fine."

Because everyone worked as a team, they soon unpacked their things into the new house with a pool in the back yard. Ally said, "Our team work made our dreams come true!"

La'Taria
Female
5th Grade

Parent Teamwork

Two little twins were in their big yellow two story house. They were playing in their house. Waiting for their dad to come home. Their mom was in the shower. Then when there dad came home he brought them a gift. Both of the wrapper were different and because they were just four years old things started to get rough.

When there dad saw them fighting he said "come on you guys they are the same thing inside." The two girls didn't listen to what their dad said. They were yelling like if they were dogs barking at an intruder. Their mom came out of the shower and saw the two little girls. Then she saw the wrappers and looked confused. She told the dad to talk to one little girl and she will talk to another.

When their parents were taking to both of them they opened their presents and showed them that it was the same. So when they told them that it was the same. So when they told each other and when the girls showed each other they were happy. After they were done saying sorry they realized that their wrappers were gone. Their parents took them so they won't fight again. So while they were playing with their new toys their mom was preparing macaroni and cheese for dinner.

L.E.A.
Female
5th Grade

Team Work

February 13, 2017, the sisters, Ally, Mary, Lola were at the airport to catch a flight to go visit their aunt Lizzie that lives in New York. They saw that their plane wasn't leaving until 12:00 in the afternoon it was barely 8:00 in the morning! One of the sisters saw that a lady that lost her passport. She was asking for help but nobody answered. She looked and looked but couldn't find it. The sisters were going on a plane to New York.

It turns out her plane was about to leave. She thought that she wouldn't be able to see her daughter this year. She kept looking, but had no luck. Ally, Mary, and Lola were going on the same plane as her. It was already 11:30 the lady then gave up and cried.

Lola felt bad so she asked the lady "what plane are you going on?"

The lady said, "the New York plane."

Lola went to her sisters and said, "We should help this lady."

Mary said, 'ARE YOU CRAZY WE DON'T EVEN KNOW HER!"

Ally said," I can't argue with Mary"

Lola said "come on girls!" It was 11:42.

At 11:45 Mary and Ally agreed because they were running out of time and they had no choice. They didn't want to let Lola down so they just agreed.

The lady was sad, but then Lola said, "You're not going to look for your passport alone. You need me and my sisters help, you need teamwork!" The lady got a smile on her face and said "Thank you!"

They looked under the seats and in the inside cafe that was nearby. They looked in the bathroom. Mary said, "NOPE NOT IN HERE BUT IT'S REALLY SMELLY!" The lady looked in her purse, but no luck. They were running out of time. It was 11:53.

"We looked everywhere," said Lola.

"No," said Ally.

"Maybe in your bags," said Mary. Then the lady looked in her bag and BOOM it was in there. It was now 11:55. "Let's hurry up ladies, we don't want to be late," said the lady. They solved the problem with team work!
THE END!

Mallory
Female
5th Grade

Chocolate Candy

Once upon a time, there were two little girls named Emmy and Elizabeth. Emmy was ten, and Elizabeth was eleven. They were the best of friends. They lived next door to each other and walked to and from school together.

One day, as they walked home from school, they came across a candy store. The girls walked into the store. As they entered, they got the good smell of the chocolate. Emmy asked the clerk, "Do you have any chocolate with caramel inside?"

The clerk replied, "Yes, I do. We just got some in an hour ago." The girls bought their chocolate and walked home. As they were walking home, they began to argue over the last piece of chocolate. They both wanted it. Emmy was holding the box, and Elizabeth snatched the box out of Emmy's hand.

Sally and Jack, Emmy's and Elizabeth's neighbors, who also walk home from school, and saw what was happening. Sally and Jack rushed over to the girls to break up the fight. Jack walked Emmy to her house, and Sally walked home with Elizabeth. Both girls told their side of the story.

The next day while walking to school, Jack tried to reason with Elizabeth. He said, "Elizabeth, I think you should apologize to Emmy." Elizabeth replied, "No way! I'm not saying sorry to her. She needs to say sorry to me."

Sally walked to school with Emmy. Sally said "Emmy, I think you should say sorry to Elizabeth." Emmy replied, "No way! I'm not saying sorry to her. She needs to say sorry to me!" When school was over, Sally and Jack talked and tried to come up with a plan to squash the beef between Emmy and Elizabeth.

Jack said, "I don't like them being mean to one another."

Sally agreed, "Yeah, neither do I. It makes me feel

sad."

Sally and Jack came up with the idea of getting the girls back to the chocolate store after school. Sally said, "I will ask Emmy to buy me chocolate, and you ask Elizabeth to buy you chocolate. Deal?" Jack agreed.

Just as Sally and Jack planned, Emmy and Elizabeth bumped into each other at the chocolate store. "What are doing here?" asked Elizabeth.

Emmy replied, "I could say the same to you."

Sally jumped in and said, "Jack and I think that you guys need to work on your problems."

Elizabeth said, "I'm not working anything out with her," and walked out.

However, Emmy said, "I'll try to work stuff out with her. It may not work but, I will still try."

Sally replied, "Thank you Emmy."

Jack said, "I will talk to Elizabeth, and try to get her to work with us."

Sally, Jack, Elizabeth, and Emmy met at a diner the following day. Jack convinced Elizabeth to talk to Emmy. Sally and Jack sat at another table. Emmy was the first to say sorry. Then Elizabeth said, " Sorry for being so mean."

Emmy replied, "It's ok" and they hugged each other.

Emmy and Elizabeth thanked Jack and Sally for helping them restore their friendship. Sally laughed, "It wasn't us, it was teamwork that helped you guys to become friends again."

They all put their hands together and shouted "Teamwork makes the dream work!"

The End

Mariah
Female
5th Grade

Teamwork Makes the Dream work

Once upon a time a little girl woke up for school. She got dressed, brushed her teeth, and washed her face. After that she ate cereal for breakfast and her mom was about to take her to school. When they were walking out the door ready to leave, mom gave her the lunch. The daughter had a big play to go to.

When the mom was driving the car it stopped right at the corner. The mom started crying because they really needed help. So the mom shouted, "Help, help somebody please help!"
Then somebody came to help them.

Two big, strong men came to help. They were hustlers named Sean and Johnnie. Sean and Johnnie told the mother that she needed to help them push the car in order to get her daughter to school on time. The mom looked sideways at her daughter and said, "If you want to get to school in time for your play you have to help me push." Then the mother said, "On the count of three." Then they all shouted, "One, two, and three!" They pushed the car to the gas station. The little girl said, "Teamwork makes the dream work." But something just wasn't right.

The mom got gas and took her daughter to school. Once the little girl arrived to school, she noticed that everyone had already changed back to their regular clothes. The little girl began to cry. Her teacher said, "What's the matter?" "I didn't get to participate in the play!" sobbed the little girl.

The rest of the students heard what the little girl told the teacher. One student said, "We will perform the play again, just for you!" The same student said, "Everyone, put your costumes back on." The class performed the play again. The little girl said, "Teamwork makes the dream work". This time it felt right.

The end

Rhea
Female
5th Grade

The Life of School

Everyone knows how it feels to sit in a chair for 8 hours. It's boring right? Well, too bad, you still have to go to school. There may be mean teachers, or maybe some nice ones. No matter what, you still have to respect them. When you work in groups you might have to work with people you don't like. However, don't pay any attention to them. Just get your work done. If you get bullied at school about random things go tell a teacher or an adult.

If you don't have good food at your school bring your own food from home. Don't make a big deal about it. Stay in school, don't be a high school dropout. When you're making projects for a science fair or black history project, you need to help each other out. Teamwork is a good thing when you work with the right people. When using teamwork you can learn new things that you didn't even know about. It can also help you learn to work with people that you don't know. You must also respect yourself, your teachers, and friends.

Anonymous

Rock, Paper, Scissors

Once there were three friends named Rock, Paper and Scissor. They needed to make a school project so they went to the store and got some equipment. That same day, there was a storm outside.

The Rock, Paper and Scissor dropped the equipment. The Scissor was cutting plants angrily, the Paper was rubbing itself on the ground, and the Rock was hitting walls.

However, after a little while they came up with an idea. They gathered regular paper for the base of the project, rocks to put on the paper, and scissors to cut out the shape.

They knew that the stuff they had put on the base were not going to stick. So, the Paper went to the store again to get some glue. However there wasn't any glue in any store! They had all run out!

The Paper thought there was a place that they had not cheeked yet. So, the Paper went home to their room, but they still did not find any glue. So, the Paper cheeked in every other room in the house, and still did not find it.

They were sad and scared, and did not want to get an "F" on their project.

Soon, it was night, and they were sitting on the porch.

Mrs. Paper brought the Rock, Paper and Scissor some cookies and milk. They ate every single thing.

The next morning, they all woke up. The Rock, Paper, and Scissor came together for breakfast.

They saw some sticky stuff falling off the tree outside. The Paper said, "We can use that for the glue!"

So they started gluing everything!

Soon, they were done, and they brought the project to school.

They showed it to the school and got an A on the project!

However, they kept in mind that with a team they can make that dream work.

Q.R.
Female
5th Grade

The Puppy Teamwork

It was a Sunday afternoon, and I was playing a game with my dad. My dad and I had a pencil and a sheet of paper that we used to keep track of our scores. Every time I won, my dad would yell, "You cheated!" even though I won fair and square.

While my dad and I were getting ready for the day, my cousin called and asked if we would come to her party. We said, "Sure, we'll be there." Finally we arrived for the party. The first thing I did was eat! I ate hamburgers, chips and guacamole. Once I finished, I had seconds! I really enjoyed the chips!

Afterwards, I went outside to play and saw some puppies trying to get out of their cage. I knew they couldn't get out because they were just little puppies. So my friends and I played outside for a little bit. When it started getting dark, we went back inside and relaxed.

Later on, we went outside to see if they could get the stuff for the fire pit. Before I could shut the door, the puppies got out of their cage and ran through the house. They were trying to get to the front door. My dad said, "Why did you let the dogs out?" I told him, "How am I supposed to know they were out?" Then everybody at the party worked as a team to get the puppies back inside their cage.

I told my dad, "I will get the door." My dad replied, "No I'll get the door!" Before we knew it, all the puppies were running towards the door, so we both closed it. Then I told my dad, "Now let's get the puppies." As a team, we put all the puppies back into their cage.

The End.

Michaela
Female
5th Grade

TEAMWORK STORY

　　Once, somewhere around the world, a kid was always messed with. Maybe just like you but couldn't fend for himself. Sometimes people would call him Jimmy Nutron because he had a big head, because of his smarts.

　　There's always a specific type of crowd, sometimes just a group of 3 people. One day, finally someone stepped up and told that crowd brought him in his group of friends and started a team to stop bullying and got more and more friends, even the bullies were his friends.

Simeion
Male
5th Grade

Soccer Life!

Back in 1st grade, at Columbia Elementary school I liked to play soccer. I don't mean I "like" to play soccer, I loved to play soccer. Soccer was my passion and I wouldn't do anything else. Whenever it was time to play outside I would always be the first in line to get the soccer ball. It was always me and my buddy Fernando out on the field. Then one day, I was late outside because I had to stay inside for 5 minutes for "moving my card" and then I saw Fernando on one team and my brother Kavali on another team. I asked to play soccer with them and I was shocked when they said "No, you need to get more people," and that's when I figured out I needed a team, desperately.

On the next day I went out to the field but this time I didn't go out to the soccer field so fast oh, no I was out on the playground looking for a team. The first person I saw was my best friend, Joshua. When I asked Joshua if he wanted to be on my team, he was thrilled as always and he said "YES!" Faster than the speed of lightning. When I asked him if he wanted to help me find more teammates he said "Yes" again and that filled me with joy. So then we set off looking for one more person so it would be equal and we could play soccer.

The next person we recruited for our team was a boy who was good at defense. The next person was another one of my good friends the person we asked to be our teammate was Da'monte. Once we asked him to be on our team at first he didn't want to do it but, eventually I bribed him with my s'more and then we had all our teammates. By the time we got to the field the game was almost over but there was still time. So I asked to play but they said there was only one more minute left so, my team and I left.

    On the next day I got my team together and we headed over to the field where the other teams were waiting. The next thing I did was something I thought I'd never do, I challenged Fernando and Kavali at the same time! Then the game was on! Fernando and his team got the ball first, but with Joshua's speed he got the ball and passed it to me from there I passed the ball to Da'monte. Da'monte started running then tripped on a rock. Then Kavali came along got the ball and started running, he was fast but he easily got distracted by a penny on the ground. I stole the ball, made the goal and we won because it was time for lunch. I was proud of myself but, mostly I was proud of my team!

The End.

Yahshua
Male
5th Grade

Teamwork Brings New Friends

Once upon a time, not long ago there was a little girl named Allisa. She had a dream to become a singer but every time she would sing two girls named Serenity and Joclyn, would bully her and say mean things to her like, "You're never going to become a singer." Even though they would say that she would always believe in herself. One day after school she saw 3 girls being bullied by Serenity and Joclyn. She saw them making fun of the 3 girls, stealing their jewelry, and eating their snacks.

Allisa walked in the conversation and screamed "That's it!" As soon as they heard her they started to laugh and said "What are you going to do to stop us? We're unstoppable." She started to stumble and replied, "It doesn't have to be like this, we could make a change." Serenity said "You are correct, I am super sorry. I guess I was just upset because no one in the school cared about me except Joclyn." "There's no reason for you to be upset. We can make this right, everything could go back to normal. Everything is much better when we work in a team. I want you to know something, teamwork makes dream work." Allisa said.

"Every day I see you do many bad things, I think about how many good things we could do together. We could make this school a better and safer place for kids to be. You're not meant to be a bad person, you have a very lovely and careful heart. Just believe in all the positive things that could happen instead of all the negative things that could happen." Allisa said. Then Joclyn busted in and said "I'm also afraid that people are going to make fun of me." Smiling, Allisa said, "Don't worry guys everything will be okay."

About three weeks later, Allisa, Serenity, and Joclyn were walking, talking, and having the time of their lives. They laughed and giggled along the way to the park. Allisa said, "So did you learn that teamwork is the key for you to succeed in life?" "Yes I did! " Said Joclyn and Serenity.

Stacy
Female
5th Grade

Teamwork Makes the Dream Work

5 Different Animals

Once upon a time there were five different animals. The animals were a pig, a dog, a horse, a goat, and a cow. One day the farm got very loud. The other animals didn't mind, but Pig did. Pig wanted to escape. He tried to escape but he couldn't. He was too fat and couldn't get through the gate. The horse saw Pig trying to get through the gate, so the horse decided to go talk to him.

The Horse said to Pig, "What are you doing?" The pig replied, "I'm trying to get through the gate because it's too loud here." The horse told Pig, "If you want you could get on my back and I could carry you over the gate. That way you'll be free." The Pig agreed.

So the pig climbed on horse's back. They both fell straight to the ground. The horse said, "You're really fat." Pig replied, "I know. I have an eating problem." So horse came up with another idea. Horse explained to pig, "Instead of getting on my back, I could open up a space through the gate and you can walk through. So the pig tried to walk through the space. Unfortunately, it was not big enough for him to walk through. The pig and the horse tried idea, after idea, but they had no luck. They tried and tried until it got dark outside. That's when they decided to go bed.

The next morning the goat saw the pig trying to get through the gate. The goat walked over and said "Are you trying to jump the gate? Because if you are, that's the wrong way." The pig said to the goat, "Well can you help me jump the gate?" The goat said, "Ok". The goat explained to the Pig, "If you are going to jump the gate we will need help from two more animals." The two animals were a cow and the dog. The pig asked the goat, "Can the horse help us out?" goat agreed. They called the horse. The pig asked the horse "Can you help me get over the gate? All of the other animals are helping me, so can you help too?" The Horse said, "Ok"

The goat gave everyone a job. The dog's job was to watch out for the farmer. The cow's job was to help the goat get the pig over the gate. The horse's job was to give the goat ideas to help the pig jump the gate. When the farmer went on his lunch break, everyone gathered to help the pig. The goat, cow and the horse all gathered around the pig. The goat said to the pig, "I want you to go all the way to the back of the gate and I want you to run as fast as you can. I want you jump when you get closer to the gate." So the pig tried, but he didn't make it over the gate.

The cow said to the pig, "Hey I have an idea! "Why don't you get on my back---."The pig stopped cow in the middle of his sentence and said, "I already tried that and it didn't go so well." The cow replied, "Oh, well it was worth a shot." Then the horse suggested, "Why don't we all make a space through the gate? Then maybe you could get through it. The pig agreed. So the cow, goat and the Horse made a space through the gate. The pig went all the way towards the back of the gate and ran as fast as he could. Finally, the pig made it through the gate, before the farmer could catch him. The pig was so happy that he yelled, "I'm free!" The pig went back to the farm and thanked all the animals for helping him. The goat said, "Well we must be very good at this kind of stuff. It's all about teamwork." Everyone was happy. Especially pig.

THE END

Victoria
Female
5th Grade

Team work in the Forest

Once upon a time there was a girl named Lilly, she loved to walk in the forest. But one day she walked way too far in the forest and she got lost. She started to wander around the area she was in, but then she found a girl. She noticed the girl was crying so she said, "What is wrong?" The other girl looked up quickly whipped her tears and said, "I'm lost!" Lilly responded "I am too and I'm not crying!"

Now they are both thinking about how they are going to get out of the forest and get home. Then something great happened Lilly had an idea, she blurted out, "I have an idea! We can use teamwork to get out of here!" Then the girl said, "That's a great idea oh, and I forgot to tell you my name, my name is Gabby" then Lilly said, "Great to know Gabby." Then the girls found a piece of paper and a pencil in the leafy dirt then they started talking about how they can draw a map of the forest.

Now they are all finished with the map so they are talking about ideas Gabby says, "We can look for a building and find a neighborhood that is next to it!" Then Lilly said, "AMAZING GABBY! You are very smart." So they found a building after many hours of walking around the forest. Then they go behind the building and find a neighborhood and both say at the same time "This is my house!" But they looked at each other confused but their faces turned into big smiles. Gabby said, 'we are neighbors?" Lilly responded, "That's a good thing!" Then they jumped into a big hug and happily into their houses. Lilly, and Gabby were happy ever after.

Victoria O.
Female
5th Grade

Teamwork

One day at a farm. There was a farmer who did not like the animals. One day the animals somehow started to talk. They said "We want freedom!" Then the leader of the animals said, "When do we want it?" "NOW!" said the rest! But the farmer was very lonely.

Then night came and it was dark out, "Go to sleep." said the farmer. "Time for our great escape!" said the pigs. So the pigs climbed over the little fence and went off. Then rooster woke up and said, "Wake up!" They all jumped up. Saying "Why did you do that rooster?"

"You do not see it the pigs are gone?" said the Rooster. "I know lets tell the farmer they are gone." Said one of the sheep. But then the farmer ran outside and said, "Where are the pigs? They are gone!" The animals shouted "We are leaving!" The Farmer said, "You all must stay!" But the animals did not care. That same night the animals planned their escaped.

The next night the last two groups of animals which were the sheep and the roosters escaped. Also the pigs came back to help. The pigs helped the sheep dig under the fence. The roosters didn't need help and they flew over the fence. Then they all went off into the forest and lived happily ever after. The farmer on the other hand had was sad at first but later found his true love with a nice lady named Liz.

Vincent
Male
5th Grade

Autographs

Autographs

Teamwork Makes the Dream Work

Autographs

Autographs

Teamwork Makes the Dream Work

Autographs

Affirmative Expression would like to congratulate the girls of Reflections for completing

The Anthology Project

and earning the prestigious title of *published authors!*

If you would like to bring **The Anthology Project** to your school, church, program, or organization please contact us!

Affirmative Expression's
Anthology Project
Turning your students into authorpreneurs!
Tierica Berry (Founder)
678.499.4405

Info@AffirmativeExpression.com
www.AffirmativeExpression.com

www.ingramcontent.com/pod-product-compliance
Lightning Source LLC
Chambersburg PA
CBHW071716040426
42446CB00011B/2083